ROCK CLIMBING
in England and Wales

ROCK CLIMBING
in England and Wales

David Simmonite

edited by

Neil Champion

NEW HOLLAND

First published in 2000 by New Holland Publishers (UK) Ltd
London · Cape Town · Sydney · Auckland

2 4 6 8 10 9 7 5 3 1

24 Nutford Place, London W1H 6DQ, United Kingdom

80 McKenzie Street, Cape Town 8001, South Africa

Level 1/Unit 4, 14 Aquatic Drive, Frenchs Forest, NSW 2086, Australia

218 Lake Road, Northcote, Auckland, New Zealand

Photographic Acknowledgements

With the exception of those listed below, all the photographs in this book were
taken by David Simmonite:

Simon Cardy p122; p123; p124 (t); p124 (b); p125; pp126–127 (c) Chris
Craggs p120 (l) Ron Kenyon p24 (tr) Alan Leary p86 (tl); p93 (tr) Simon Nadin
p66 (r) Stephen Reid p24 (tl) Carl Ryan p116 (b) Don Sargeant p108;
pp110–111 (c) Keith Sharples p64 Nigel Shepherd: p39; p152 Ian Smith p153;
p154 (l); p15 (r); p155 Sam Sturgess p116 (t) John Sumner p109; p110 (l);
p111 (r) Dave Wilkinson p30 (tl); p40; p42 (l); p49 (t); p126 (l) Ray Wood:
pp92-93 (c); p96 (l)

t = top; b = bottom; c = centre; l = left; r = right

ISBN 1 85974 408 7

Publishing Manager: Jo Hemmings
Project Editor: Mike Unwin
Copy Editor: Neil Champion
Designer & Cover Design: Alan Marshall
Cartography: William Smuts
Index: Janet Dudley
Production: Joan Woodroffe

Reproduction by Pica Colour Separation Overseas (Pte) Ltd, Singapore
Printed and bound in Singapore by Tien Wah Press (Pte) Ltd

Half-title page: Ritchie Duffy takes on a dynamic boulder problem (6c) at Bowden
Doors. Title page: Sam Whittaker on *Paralogism* (E7 6c), Upper Tier, The Roaches.
Left: Abigail May on *The Adultress* (E2 5c), Trial Wall, Rhossili Crags, Gower.
Opposite: Tim Emmett on the first ascent of *The Muppet Show* (E7 6b), Rusty
Walls, Pembroke.

This book is dedicated to my late sister, Lisa.

CONTENTS

LOCATION OF CLIMBING SITES

1 The Quiet County
2 Wasdale
3 Langdale
4 Borrowdale
5 Lancashire Quarries
6 Malham Cove
7 Almscliff
8 Ilkley
9 High Tor
10 Raven Tor
11 Eastern GritstoneEdges
12 The Roaches
13 Pen Trwyn
14 Gogarth
15 Llanberis Pass
16 Tremadog
17 Cader Idris & Craig Cywarch
18 Pembroke
19 Gower
20 Lundy
21 Avon Gorge
22 Dartmoor Tors
23 Cornish Granite
24 Conner Cove
25 Southern Sandstone

PREFACE

DAVID SIMMONITE

'Capture the moment and the atmosphere', a very good point once made to me about photography. A principle that I have followed ever since. However, photography didn't come first; no, it was a passion for the wide-open spaces and countryside that surrounded my birthplace of Sheffield. On trips out, at an early age tramping the moors and valleys, I was caught up in the beauty of landscape, it captured my imagination.

It wasn't until I left school that I became engrossed in photography. A borrowed camera was the first stage, followed by a purchase of my very own. Many images later and a long, self-taught, learning curve, I discovered the excitement of another adventure, rock climbing.

Climbing is, for some, an all-consuming pastime and maybe it is for me. I glow when I think about my first tentative efforts on Stanage gritstone. It does occasionally have its downsides but it has given me a great deal of satisfaction and self-belief; many good friendships have been formed along the way. I feel very lucky to have discovered climbing. It has helped me through dark periods in my life, given copious highlights and has always been a constant, a form of escape from everyday stresses.

It was inevitable that photography and climbing would become intertwined and so began the path I have chosen to pursue, some say to obsession, I say with enthusiasm. Blending these two, demands an immense amount

Above: *David Simmonite on a 7a+ boulder problem at Fontainebleau, France*

of hard work and commitment. It involves taking on two different challenges at the same time in an attempt to be in the right place to capture that fleeting moment when everything comes together.

In the pursuit of material for this book, endless hours (and miles travelled) have been spent in the search for the right light, angle and atmosphere that will bring out the best of each crag or area. I lost count of the days when the light or conditions were not right; these could be seen as wasted days but how can that be when you are in places that you love. Many, many people have helped and contributed, showing the great community spirit that exists in climbing.

This book is an attempt to show my vision and passion for the places in England and Wales where I have travelled. I hope it gives an insight into the splendour and excitement of a world seen through my eyes. I try to communicate the reason why people climb in the first place. Compiling a book like this is never easy and many climbers will wonder where is their favourite crag or climb? With an area as large and diverse as England and Wales there are inevitable omissions for which I can only apologise. But then no two climbers would ever agree on what to include, and unfortunately there is never space for everything. I hope that by looking at the images in this book and reading the compelling personal accounts, you will gain the same thrill and satisfaction that I do and will become similarly inspired.

FOREWORD

RON FAWCETT

What a brief, to pictorially illustrate what is rock climbing in England and Wales. David's images take us on a journey from the well-known venues like the harsh gritstone of Yorkshire where I learned my craft, to esoteric gems on southern sandstone, epic routes on the island of Lundy, and valleys such as Llanberis in North Wales and Wasdale in the Lake District, that are impregnated with history and mystery in magnificent mountain settings. In this epic journey we are privileged to see the like of Dave Birkett on his Pavey Ark masterpiece *Impact Day* and the immaculate *Terrier's Tooth* on Chair Ladder. Here is something for us all to be inspired by, no matter what grade we are climbing at or where we hail from. We are lucky in this small isle of ours to have such a diversity of rock types and venues. This is amply demonstrated by comparing the shots of Ilkley Quarry's somewhat urban setting with the stark majesty of Gogarth on Anglesey. We are also blessed with a multitude of climbing styles, from the social top-roping at Harrison's Rocks, sport climbing at Pen Trwyn, magical bouldering on Dartmoor or phenomenal adventures on Cornish sea cliffs. I wish there were more days in the week.

Above: *Ron Fawcett bouldering at his second home, The Plantation, Stanage Edge.*
Opposite: *Dave Henderson on Don't Stop Now, Dartmoor.*

As a climber I am often asked what is the biggest thing I have climbed? But what is mere size? Size is definitely not everything – look at those images of the frozen waves of sandstone that is Northumberland or the intriguing beauty of a gritstone boulder. David understands this. He looks and most often finds and captures the essential qualities of a place – no easy thing to do, but far more rewarding than merely looking for the height of a route.

We are fortunate in this book to have local knowledge in the form of introductions to each venue by characters who are passionate about their areas. Be it in the celebration of some wild place or in a man-made hole in the ground. They are all precious and if this book gives you the inspiration to go and search out some of these venues, then it has more than done its job.

Even after all these years of climbing I am still excited by it – it is so much more than just a pastime. Sometimes it hurts, sometimes it scares me, but above all I love it. What has drawn me to David's work is that he shares and expresses that same love of the rock – it shines through from this marathon project. David's perception of what English and Welsh climbing is all about should strike a chord in us all.

Ron Fawcett has been climbing for the past thirty years, for the last twenty of which it has been his profession. He has climbed and pioneered new routes from the U.S.A. to the Far East. He has been the subject of several climbing T.V. documentaries and programmes, and has written for climbing magazines and lectured all over the World. He lives in Hathersage in the Peak District below his adopted gritstone edges with his wife and two children.

INTRODUCTION

Climbing in England and Wales has deep roots – maybe none deeper. Reputedly the first piece of rock climbed by a mountaineer purely for the sheer enjoyment and exhilaration of the dance, took place in the English Lake District. The year was 1886, the climber one W P Haskett-Smith, and the rock, the now famous Napes Needle on the flanks of Great Gable in Wasdale. It didn't lead to the top of some prized summit. The 20 metre route didn't really lead anywhere as such – except into the history books as marking the birth of rock climbing as its own sport, as opposed to Alpinism or Mountaineering.

From this point onwards the mountains, crags and sea-cliffs of England and Wales were to be explored and opened up for what they had to offer in their own right, rather than as providing pre-Alpine training routes for the privileged middle and upper class members of London's Alpine Club who had their sights set on higher things in Switzerland and France.

The great pioneers of the early period (O G Jones, Norman Collie, the Abraham brothers, J W Puttrell, Fred Botterill, J M Archer Thomson, to name but a few) had the place to themselves and all that rock to explore to their heart's content. They gravitated to the mountain venues of Snowdonia and the Lake District. They met at Easter and other times at the Pen y Gwryd inn, Capel Curig, North Wales, and the Wasdale Head Inn, deep in the heart of the Lakes. From these bases, they could get in amongst the hills in short time to tease out the gullies and cracks that yielded the climbs of the day. In 1898, the Climbers' Club was founded to cater for the needs and aspirations of these men. It was to bring together the

Above: *Today's modern climbing equipment is a far cry from that used by the sport's earliest pioneers.*

Opposite: *John Dunne grapples with his mind-blowing route, Big Issue (E9 6c), Bosherston Head, Pembroke.*

threads of English and Welsh climbing at that point in time. Guidebooks were to follow, the first ever produced for rock climbs. These included O G Jones's *Rock Climbing in the English Lake District*, 1897 (in which Jones first proposed the adjectival grading system of Easy, Moderate, Difficult, Severe, and so on, later adopted throughout the country), and George Abraham's equally important *Rock-climbing in North Wales*, published in 1906.

And make no mistake, although relatively small in size and area, the rock climbing playgrounds that were being developed and talked about at the turn of the 20th century by their enthusiasts, showed enormous variety, complexity and all the challenge that could be wished for. One of the greatest Cumbrian climbs of all time, *Central Buttress* on Scafell, has eight pitches of the highest quality, up to 5b in technical grade. It fell to S W Herford and G S Sansom in 1914. No mean feat.

Cornish Granite was climbed early on by A W Andrews, and exploration started to take place on the

Above: *The powerful Neil Bentley bouldering on* Ben's Roof *deep in the cave at Raven Tor.*

Gritstone edges of Derbyshire, Staffordshire and Yorkshire. Limestone took a little longer to catch on, but catch on it did. The relentless opening up of new venues by each successive generation, along with pushing the technical grade of climbing, was to become a feature of the sport throughout this century.

Here at the start of a new millenium, that truth is still with us, as this celebratory book can testify. The routes whose first struggles are lost or etched in the rock itself, combine with the new and great climbs of today. Weather still interferes, as it always will on this damp little island, providing moments of utter frustration and disbelief; and of course, total joy when clouds hold back longer than expected and that coveted climb is snatched just in time. That is all part of the English and Welsh climbing experience. Small wonder that the pioneers started off in the damp, dark mountain gullies where the weather has little inlfuence on the outcome.

The main changes between then and now involve equipment, ethics, training, expectations, and of course grades. The sport has sub-divided giving rise to aid climbing, bouldering, sport climbing, indoor competitions – traditional climbing is but one more on the list. Today we choose how we play the game. As the years have rolled by, the grades have inevitably gone up – climbing has got harder. At first, equipment helped to make the leaps – reliable rope, better protection, sticky rubber boots, chalk – all ushered in on a wave of controversy, now accepted as the norm. Today, training and focus are the order – a new professionalism marks those at the cutting edge of the sport.

Debates about the ethics of climbing style have been part of the climbing scene since the very beginning. The

Above: *Jibé Tribout tries out* Deliverance *(6c), at the Plantation, Stanage Edge.*

Above: *Percy Bishton takes a lob off his own* Rowley Birkin QC *(E6 6c), at Higgar Tor.*

use of pegs and bolts, inspecting climbs by abseil before doing them; even gardening and placing protection before the lead; practising the moves on a top rop; chipping holds – all these tactics come from the depths of time, rather than being invented just the other day for use on some gnarly reputation-making E8. In growing and evolving, the sport has not left its roots behind. It has carried the good as well as the bad with it. It has fragmented, priorities have changed, it has become infinitely more complex. But as the poets would have it, the eye changing changes all.

Hopefully, some great measure of enjoyment still lies at the heart of it all. Certainly, that comes through in David Simmonite's awesome images and the unique testimonies of our authors, where that word memory crops up again and again. It's a factor in our enjoyment. We remember, we relive the route, we try to come to terms with its meaning,

we discuss in the pub afterwards, we even mythologise (well, we're allowed to, aren't we?).

Memorable things and events are perhaps becoming increasingly rare in our pensioned society, like the wild places we seem to long for and need. But you don't forget the fear and the fight of your first lead, your first Extreme, your first flight. More valuable than gold and maybe something that you can take with you. At least the memories are yours, and can be shared free of charge – the shared memories of the history of the rock that we inherit, and the personal memories of the routes that have marked us.

Routes humble and routes horrendous, they are all here in this inspired collection. Words and images loaded with personal meaning – but hopefully shared out for us all to appreciate and to remind us of our own days out there on crag, coastal cliff or mountain route.

THE QUIET COUNTY

JOHN EARL

Northumberland, the Quiet County, is situated in the North East of England sandwiched between industrial Tyneside and the rolling hills of the Scottish Borders. I say quiet – that is the way it was and to some extent still is when compared to the Peak District and the Yorkshire Dales. However, it is certainly becoming more popular as climbers discover the charm of its quality rock and varied climbing, in a beautiful and tranquil setting. But the meadow turf at the foot of Bowden and the thick bed of pine needles which once cushioned the landings at Kyloe, are being replaced by the ubiquitous bouldering mat – which it must be said, is quite a good conservation feature!

There is a good variety of rock – igneous dolerite (known locally as Whin Sill) at Crag Lough and Peel Crag, volcanic at Henhole Crag in the Cheviots. But the rock for which the county is now best known is sandstone.

The in-vogue crags are in the Bowden Doors and Kyloe groups which provide excellent short routes, micro routes and boulder problems on generally good quality sandstone. Good quality that is, when soloing or leading and therefore taking care, and being as one with the rock. Under these circumstances very little breaks or crumbles. However, when top-roping (which is frowned upon) and therefore probably not exercising the same degree of care, or flying through the air hoping for a runner to hold, the rock is perhaps a tad less reliable. The bottom of Tiger's Wall at Bowden is testimony to over-ambitious and optimistic leaders who relied too much on their 'Friends' behind thin flakes.

Bowden is a fantastic place to solo or boulder. It faces West, gets most of what is going in terms of sunshine and has superb views of the Cheviot Hills. But the visitors who restrict themselves to the Bowden and Kyloe crags miss out on many of the county's classics which are to be found at Ravensheugh, Simonside, Wanneys, and Callerheus to name but a few. So if you enjoy three star routes of superb quality in fantastic settings shared only with the grouse, leave the crowds at Bowden and Kyloe and head for the hills. If you are really unlucky, you might have to share it with me.

John Earl has climbed regularly for over thirty years, throughout the UK and Europe, participating in all aspects of rock climbing – traditional, sport and bouldering. He has pioneered new routes in Northumberland, the Lake District, Yorkshire and Scotland.

He has been involved in the last three guidebooks to climbing in Northumberland, and is currently editing the first guide to bouldering in the county. He was also co-author of the FRCC guide to the Eastern Crags.

Above: *Steve Crowe and Richie Duffy discuss* The Manta (E2 6a)*.*

Opposite: *Keith Ashton on* Tiger's Wall (VS 5a)*, Bowden Doors*

Above: *Lucy Atkinson on the superb* The Trial *(E2 5c), Bowden Doors.*

Right: *Steve Crowe on* Poseidon Adventure *(E4 6a), Bowden Doors.*

Below: *Karin Magog on a 6a boulder problem at Bowden Doors.*

Left: *Ritchie Duffy on* The Manta *(E2 6a),* Bowden Doors.

Below left: *Helen Fawcett climbing* The Scoop *(VS 4b), Bowden Doors.*

Below right: *Percy Bishton on* Lost Cause *(E4 6b), Back Bowden Doors.*

Opposite: *Karin Magog climbing the classic and sought-after* Tube *(E4 5c), Back Bowden Doors.*

WASDALE

IAIN TURNBULL

One of the first thoughts you might have on arriving in Wasdale is that the scale seems different to the rest of the Lake District. In reality, the mountains are only just bigger than some neighbours. But climbing here serves only to reinforce that impression. As you drive down the narrow road leading into the valley, eyes stray to the steep, rugged slopes of Scafell, Scafell Pike and Great Gable. High up on these slopes are the crags and buttresses that not only gave birth to the sport of rock climbing over a hundred years ago, but still today provide the modern climber with that same challenge and thrill experienced by those Victorian explorers.

Great Gable, with its distinctive pyramid profile and crags near the summit, dominates the head of the valley. Its crags and ridges provided early climbers with some of the finest routes in the country, and through the growing influence of photography, many more people were able to see the attractions of these wild places. In the time since the first photographs of Napes Needle appeared in London newspapers with an account of the first ascent by W P Haskett-Smith in 1886, many more climbers have made their contribution to this valley and to the styles and ethics of British rock climbing, to make it the sport we know today.

Above: *The long walk up Gavel Neese onto Great Gable, with Wasdale down below.*

Opposite: *Mike Weeks on Kern Knotts West Buttress (MVS 4b), Great Gable.*

Anyone setting out for a day's climbing in Wasdale now has a huge choice of routes and venues – steep, exposed multi-pitch adventures on Scafell's East Buttress; catching the evening sun on Central Buttress; smaller crags of Buckbarrow and Kern Knotts, which may be dry when the tops are covered in cloud. Not everyone will relish the long drive from a main road, or the long walk-ins to these mountain settings. But if you are looking for adventure, a sense of place with a true history, a feeling of remoteness and somewhere that still has potential for new things to happen in, then Wasdale is for you. These are some of the reasons why for me Wasdale has always felt just that little bit bigger.

Iain Turnbull was brought up in a village just a few miles from Wasdale. He began climbing at the age of 13 in the valley, and has continued to do so, putting up new routes. He enjoys all aspects and grades of climbing, from Diff to E6, traditional to sport. He owns a climbing and canoeing shop in Keswick. He has climbed throughout Britain, Europe and Thailand.

Above: *Is this where it all began? Well, maybe. Iain Turnbull belays Mike Weeks on* Wasdale Crack *(HS 4b), Napes Needle, Great Gable, Wasdale.*

Left: *Iain Turnbull on* Brown Badger *(E5 6a), Kern Knotts, Great Gable, Wasdale.*

Above: *A misty view from Mickledore past Scafell Crag towards Wasdale.*

Above left: *Jim Roberts on pitch four of one of the longest routes in the Lake District,* Lord of the Rings *(E2 5a, 5c, 5b, 5b, 5b, 5a, 4c, 5b, 4b, 4c, 5b, 5a, 4c),* Wasdale.

Opposite: *Russell Dicks climbing in far from ideal (but typical mountain) weather –* The Buckbarrow Needle, *(VS 4b, 4c),* Buckbarrow, Wasdale.

Left: *Iain Turnbull, Adam Hocking and Russell Dicks watching bad weather coming in from Buckbarrow, Wasdale.*

LANGDALE

DAVE BIRKETT

Hiking up the fellside towards Pavey Ark and trying to keep up with your grandfather, who's carrying a heavy metal bar for an anchor and an old cart rope, is not everyone's first experience of cragging in the Lakes. Being lowered down rock steps onto small grassy ledges to catch sheep which have got stuck, and then being pulled back up by my grandfather was probably mine. This may not be the best way to start rock climbing, but at the age of eleven I didn't know anything about climbing, rope strengths or belays. All I knew is that it was fun and well worth the walk-in.

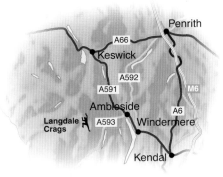

I still don't know if it was just my childhood experiences that have given me a great love for climbing in the Lakes or the sheer number of brilliant routes, the history of the classic climbs or the quality of the rock. Maybe it's just the beauty of the fells themselves. It's probably a combination of these factors for most people and everyone will have their own favourite route and crag – be it the roadside desperate in Borrowdale, or multi-pitch scrambles on Scafell and classics in the Langdale valley. The Lakes has so much to offer to climbers of all grades although I feel, for the greatest rewards, not being afraid of long walk-ins or the cold is a must. It's hard to believe that even on the finest of summer days you can have the mountain crags to yourself. I know I prefer it that way but you can't help feeling sorry for the people who just couldn't be bothered to walk up the hill. Maybe if my grandfather hadn't dragged me out into the fells so many times as a child I'd also find the walks too much effort.

But just one day's climbing on Scafell is worth ten on any other crag. The sad thing is that some summers, one day is all you get on the high crags. This can be very frustrating when you're trying to climb some of the last great unclaimed lines in the area, which to me has become a bit of an obsession in recent years. I think that people have always been climbing the last few great lines and I guess they always will. Luckily the further away from the road, the more there are, so in the Lakes there are still quite a few. I have had a look at most of these routes and they all have one thing in common. Yes – too bloody hard and dangerous.

So then you need to spend more time, generally alone, rehearsing the moves and looking for gear, if there is any, all the time knowing that some day soon you will have to lead this route.

It's this time alone on the crags that I love the most. Perhaps being in the Lakeland fells makes me feel at one with myself. All I know is that it's still fun in spite of the dangers.

Above: *Looking up to Raven Crag in Langdale, one of the most beautiful mountain settings in the English Lake District.*

Opposite: *Dave Birkett tackling the crux sequence of his own route, Impact Day (E9 6c), Pavey Ark, Langdale.*

Dave Birkett, 31, has been climbing for 12 years (in South Africa, Europe, North America and Asia). Born in Langdale, he still lives in the valley. He is best known for his hard, unprotected, traditional routes in the Lake District, including If Six was Nine *(E9 6c),* Impact Day *(E9 6c) and* Bleed in Hell *(E8 6c)*

Opposite: Tom Mathews belays as Jo Scott climbs the third pitch of The Crack *(VS 4b, 4c, 4c), Gimmer Crag, Langdale.*

Right: *Mary Jenner arranges protection on Spring Bank (E1 5c), Gimmer Crag, Langdale.*

Below: *Alan Leary climbs above his belayer, Sam Sturgess, on the third pitch of Kipling Groove (HVS -, 4c, 5a), Gimmer Crag, Langdale.*

Above: *Helen Board belays as Steve Bunston climbs the second pitch of* Haste Not *(VS 4b, 4c, 4b), White Ghyll Crag, Langdale.*

Left: *Dave Birkett stands above his own route,* Impact Day *(E9 6c) on Pavey Ark, Langdale.*

Opposite: *Graham Lee climbing the first pitch of* Astra *(E2 5c, 4c) on Pavey Ark, Langdale, with Mary Jenner providing the belay.*

BORROWDALE

COLIN DOWNER

With over 70 crags to choose from, Borrowdale has much to recommend it to the local and visiting climber alike. Much of its appeal lies in the great variety it yields – single and multi-pitch routes of all grades. No Borrowdale climbing trip would be complete without a visit to Shepherd's Crag. A glut of quick-drying, easy and middle grade classics, along with the easy access, ensures the enduring popularity of this crag. Then there is Reecastle tucked away in the Watendlath Valley, perfectly situated to catch the last rays of the evening sun. This fearsome crag, though small, packs a mighty punch, boasting some of the valley's, if not the entire Lake District's, hardest routes. On such steep, strenuous rock, strong fingers are essential. And where better to get them than the remarkable Bowderstone, its underbelly covered with torturous boulder problems? Its popularity with tourists means that the dedicated local climbers that frequent it are often accompanied by curious onlookers, the odd bright spark pointing out the ladder as an easier means of ascent. With such a diversity of crags, ideal equally for leisurely summer afternoons as for the frantic dash to snatch a route after work on unpromising autumn evenings, the valley has something for everyone.

Above: *The well-known Shepherd's Cafe in Borrowdale.*

Opposite: *James McHaffie climbing* The Grasper *(E1 5b), at Shepherd's Crag in Borrowdale.*

Borrowdale has always been firmly on the climbing map, but the most definitive moment in its history came in 1974, when a new age of Lakeland climbing began. 'The man who transforms The Great Buttress (Goat Crag) from a peg route to a free route,' said Ross & Thompson's early pirate guide, 'is sure of his niche in climbing history.' Sure enough, Pete Livesey's visionary ascent of this previously aided climb produced the superb *Footless Crow*, not only raising the standard of Lakeland climbing but opening people's minds to what was possible on other areas of steep, uncompromising rock. This and other ascents of a similar standard raised Borrowdale's profile and led to climbing's answer to the Gold Rush. This flurry of activity led to the number of crags listed in the guide doubling in 22 years, and new discoveries are still being made.

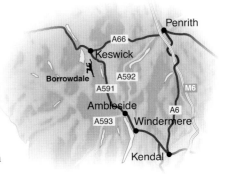

One pioneer is the indefatigable Ray McHaffie, who has been making a steady onslaught on Borrowdale rock since his first route in 1962. Nearly 40 years on he is still going strong and his formidable efforts have yielded some gems. He is also a valued regular of the hub of Borrowdale's climbing fraternity, Shepherd's Cafe, and can be found on many a summer's afternoon dispensing his wisdom to the heady accompaniment of Barbara's cakes and Martin's esoteric charm.

Colin Downer has been climbing in the Lakes for far more years than he cares to remember. He has been responsible for the discovery of over one hundred new routes and several new crags and is still going strong.

Above: *Adam Hocking on* Kransic Crack Direct *(HVS 5a), Shepherd's Crag, Borrowdale.*

Left: *George Rea on* Guillotine *(E2 5c), Reescastle Crag, Borrowdale.*

Right: *Adam Hocking performs* Daylight Robbery *(E5 6c) at Reescastle Crag, Borrowdale.*

Above: *Adam Hocking on the second ascent of* Bleed in Hell *(E8 6c), Bowderstone Crag, Borrowdale.*

Left: *Outrageous moves by Adam Hocking on* Bleed in Hell *(E8 6c), Bowderstone Crag, Borrowdale.*

Right: *Gareth Parry powers up* De Quincy *(E7 6b), Bowderstone Crag, Borrowdale.*

LANCASHIRE QUARRIES

GARETH PARRY

Lancashire has for a long time been considered something of a backwater in British climbing, an esoteric gem, a place for adventure. In reality it is a place where real climbers are made. People who have not visited it can have no feeling for the place, and it can have no meaning or life for them. But for many who have been there, it forms the basis of their climbing life and love of climbing.

Lancashire climbing thrives now, continuing to go from strength to strength. It has usually managed to keep up with pace of development elsewhere in the country but this is not where its strength has lain. It has acted as more of a breeding ground of talent than a forcing ground of grades. It has no cliques, no gangs, no groups, it has climbers, real climbers from every generation who have one thing in common – they love to climb.

A list of past masters of the Lancashire quarries reads like a who's who of British climbing. The quarries have become a place in which many a young and up and coming rock star has cut his or her teeth. The likes of Cronshaw, Lonsdale, Edwards, Fawcett and notably Pasquill in the '60s and '70s, and Leach and Pritchard in the '80s. Hopefully the '90s will be remembered for what Ian Vickers and I myself managed to achieve in and around the Wilton Quarries. For the future, we now stand on the verge of a new era. Adam Dewhurst and Ryan Pasquill represent the modern face and future of not just Lancashire but climbing in Britain as a whole. Ryan, probably the first son of an original '70s rock star, has finally come of age to find himself a major player in the future of British rock climbing. The pair of them have managed to successfully bring together the two varying disciplines of competition climbing and traditional climbing, proving to the critics that the two can exist in a happy balance.

So why do I still love climbing in the quarries? I suppose it has it all. The lines, the cracks, the aretes, the big blank walls and the unclimbed walls. But it's not just the climbing, it's more than that; it's part of the backbone of rock climbing in this country, it's part of the history and it will always be a part of me.

Lancastrian Gareth Parry is 26 and has been climbing for 14 years, having taught himself the ropes.

Above: *An unknown climber perched high on a Tangerine Trip (E3 5c), Anglezarke.*

Opposite: *Gareth Parry on the first ascent of Toxic Billberries (E8 7a), Wilton One.*

Above: *Graham Sutton climbs* Central Route (E1 5b), Wilton One. *This is one of the many excellent routes at Wilton Quarries.*

Left: *Keith Phizacklea takes on* New Jerusalem (E4 6a), Anglezarke.

Opposite: *Martin Crocker, the well-known South-West activist, on* Parasite (E5 6b), Wilton One.

MALHAM COVE

NEIL FOSTER

Malham Cove forms a spectacular natural amphitheatre, dominating the head of Airedale in the Yorkshire Dales. Approaching on the tourist footpath alongside Malham Beck, the scale of the cliff is hard to gauge. Trees mask the view as the dominant Central Wall draws near, then gawping crowds of pre-picnic daytrippers appear, standing around the eerie resurgence at the base of the Cove. Join them and look up at the impending walls, overhanging in the middle for an unbroken height of over 60m. You cannot fail to be impressed.

The Central Wall is home to some of the best sport climbs in the country, most starting from The Catwalk, a convenient narrow ledge perched above the beck. On the left is *Yosemite Wall*, a line of dramatic undercut flakes, Central Wall's most obvious weakness. To the right are small pitches and big extensions and projects, with enough stars to satisfy the most discerning.

Don't miss *Mescalito* with its fingery start, powerful undercutting sequence and perplexing headwall. To the right *Zoolook* is still much sought-after, but *Controversy* is a giant of a pitch, inspiring some of the most protracted sieges ever witnessed on Yorkshire limestone. Upstairs, *Obsession*, a vision-ary route, attracts many with its sustained and intricate wall climbing on perfect rock.

The Left Wing, apparently insignificant, hosts a series of miniature test-pieces. The Right Wing is the traditional play-ground and offers brilliant routes from VS to E5. The Carnage Headwall features the best rock in the Cove, but the trio of *Wombat*, *Slender Loris* and *Doubting Thomas* are my favourites. Pull through the roof on *Doubting Thomas* and in an instant the position is so strenuous that a clock begins to tick. Success or failure depends on just how quickly the hidden holds can be located, the runners arranged, and the awful truth that those are indeed the finishing holds be recognised and accepted. The clock beats many on first acquaintance.

Finally, The Terrace features short pitches on excellent rock above an awesome void, giving them an impact out of all propor-tion to their modest length. *Butch Cassidy*, *Wild West Hero* and *Midnight Cowboy* are all enjoyable outings, particularly the last, with its steep start, technical rampline and powerful finishing flake.

Neil Foster started climbing in 1978 on the limestone crags and quarries in North Lancashire, and in the Lake District and Yorkshire Dales. He has climbed extensively around Britain, as well as in New Zealand, America, and Europe. He has contributed to several guidebooks, including writing the Malham Cove chapter in the classic 1985 Yorkshire Limestone *guide. He has written the Rock Notes column in* High *magazine for the last 12 years. Neil lives in Tideswell in the Peak District, a good base to enjoy his passion for powerful gritstone. Today he favours mountain crags and sea cliffs.*

Above: *The great amphitheatre of Malham Cove.*

Opposite: *Lucy Creamer on Mescalito (F7c+), Malham Cove.*

Above: *Peter Robins on* Doubting Thomas *(E5 6b), Right Wing, Malham Cove.*

Above left: *Ben Bransby does the* Bongo Fury *(F7b), Lower Tier, Malham Cove.*

Opposite: *Adam Dewhurst in a superb and exposed position, while feeding his* Obsession *(F7b+), Upper Tier, Malham Cove.*

Left: *Adam Dewhurst caught on a* Bolt Revolt *(E3 6a), Lower Tier, Malham Cove.*

Opposite: *Lucy Creamer belays Ian Vickers on* Seventh Aardvark *(F7b), Lower Tier, Malham Cove.*

Right: *Adrian Wood falling off* The Groove *(F8a+), Malham Cove.*

Below: *Lucy Creamer, one of Britain's top women climbers, showing the way to overcome hard moves on* Mescalito *(F7c+), Lower Tier, Malham Cove.*

ALMSCLIFF

ANDY BOWMAN

It is where it began – 25 years ago. I leafed through the plastic-bound guidebook and matched the dotted line with the features on the rock face in front of me. I tightened the Hawkins walking boots and climbed the leaning flake. My first official route. I ran down to the side of Low Man, speedily picked up the guidebook and realised the next climb was a Very Difficult, so immediately set off upwards, slower this time, as it was steeper. I lost balance and wavered outwards but held the top with a smile and rush of re-charged blood. The rest of the day I spent solving the puzzle of guidebook and route and rapidly climbing again and again to the top of Almscliff Crag. There was no complicated thought in my head, just a natural, simple and totally pure, relaxing, movement over the rock, isolated from everything in this vacuum.

The previous week I had watched a TV documentary on Everest. I realised that to climb high mountains I would have to climb properly. Years of hiking, camping and youth hostelling had been adventurous, but it would have to get more serious before I could take on Everest. So here I was, learning to rock climb at Almscliff.

Many others had been there before me – Slingsby, Frankland, Dolphin and Austin. It is a well-known landmark for anyone travelling north from Leeds. It dominates the broad sweep of Wharfedale; your eyes are drawn to it perched up on the valley side. We often played there as kids in and around the many chimneys, gullies and rifts. But I and other climbers were to grow to appreciate it in a more intimate way. The crag had a Tor-like appearance with no clean smooth dominant lines, but a collection of complex features – steep with round bold cracks yet walls and slabs offering an infinite variety of holds which give the climber the perfect rock to climb, iron hard, and the options are endless. I have moved away from the area now, but whenever I visit the family in Leeds or pass en route to the north I make a visit to the crag, climb some routes or maybe take on the boulder problems I now know so well – familiar movements, sometimes different, always steep, the holds haven't changed in 25 years, the view is still the same. I will do the same for the next 25 years; it is where it began, it's where it will end.

Above: *Cows relaxing amongst the rural delights of Almscliff Crag.*

Opposite: *Keith Ashton soloes Fence Buttress (VS 5b), Almscliff.*

Andy Bowman is 41 and has climbed for over 25 years. Venues include Almscliff, Yorkshire, Lakes, Scotland, throughout Europe, USA and the Himalaya. He enjoys bouldering, rock climbing, ice climbing, big walls, winter and summer to grade VII ice; E6; F7c+; VI big walls; Ed Sup. He has worked in teaching, at climbing shops, and for Wild Country, and is currently Boreal and Mammut UK agent.

ILKLEY

JOHN DUNNE

Yorkshire Gritstone has long been a forcing ground for generations of new route pioneers: Arthur Dolphin, Allan Austin, Pete Livesey, Al Manson, Ron Fawcett and me, John Dunne. It has a unique character that attracts climbers of all grades. From classic Severes on Brimham's rough, rounded grit, to the steep, unforgiving cracks of Almscliff and Ilkley. My fondest memories are of Ilkley, home to some of gritstone's best routes – *A Climb*, a three-pitch Severe, and my own *The New Statesman*, E8 7a.

Above: *The Cow (on the left) and Calf (the boulder on the right) at Ilkley.*

Opposite: *Nick Fletcher on Tufted Crack (E1 5c), The Quarry, Ilkley.*

I started climbing at Ilkley at the age of eleven. My first routes were often soloed because of my lack of equipment. I still remember walking into the quarry, looking at *Wellington Crack* (E4) and dreaming of the day that I would be good enough to climb it. I would watch in awe as many climbers tried and failed to tame this fierce 15 metre finger crack. Several years later, with butterflies in my stomach, I stood with a rack of borrowed gear ready to attempt to realise my dream.

I placed the first small wire and reversed back down. Up to now the main crack had always appeared the most difficult but the first layback threw me off slightly by its awkwardness, requiring power and faith in friction. My battered rock shoes were slipping on the smooth quarried grit. The second wire went in well. Whilst shaking out, I reasoned that I could place a lot of gear and pump out, or I could make a dash for the rest before the crux. Indecision a few feet further found me placing more gear than I really needed and my arms rapidly becoming heavy. Reaching the shake-out, I tried desperately to de-pump, but I knew that however much I recovered, there would not be enough to see me to the top. I shook out for as long as I could before starting the crux sequence. As soon as I began to layback my arms went dead. I pulled through into the top crack, my arms wilting by the second. Reaching a good finger-lock, I placed what I knew would be my last piece of gear and went for it. Two moves short of the top I came off, taking a 6 metre fall. Dreams of a clean ascent vanished as I lowered to the ground. I had become one of the many who had tried and failed on *Wellington Crack*. One week later, I climbed the route first go. My ascent of *Wellington Crack* remains one of the best climbing days of my life.

Since exploding onto the scene in the early '80s, John Dunne has remained at the forefront of British climbing. His list of first ascents contains many of the hardest routes in Britain, including Divided Years *(E10 7a),* Widdop Wall *(E9 7a),* Big Issue *(E9 6c),* Carmen Picasso *(E9 6c),* New Statesman *(E8 7a) and many more.*

HIGH TOR

MALCOLM TAYLOR

Every time I passed below High Tor, it frightened me to death. It still does, in a way. It lurks far above the river, beguiling and bald and bigger than it should be, the most impressive roadside crag in the country. The startling exposure and the fear it induces and our ability to control it – or not – makes High Tor one of the great places to climb. Since I first plucked up the courage to venture on to the main face the crag has been central to my love of climbing, and central to the many memories it has given me...

Topping-out on *Darius*, the best E2 in England, to be greeted by two police officers, alerted by a passing motorist to a climber stuck on the face – a well-known climber who wasn't stuck at all, who hadn't even fallen off, but who had a reputation for climbing slowly.

Hanging gratefully from the creaking pegs atop the first pitch of *Castellan*, chuffed to bits at having done it without anything like a jump, patiently belaying as my heavy gritstone-aficianado friend struggled to aid his way across the roof. He became hopelessly entangled in the ropes, the sloping ledge dug fiercely into my backside. We ended up benighted and forced to abseil and in the gloom we left trousers and shoes at the foot of the route, folded neatly as though for room service to collect.

A glorious autumnal day on the left wing, my wife and I had the crag to ourselves. We climbed six of the area's E4s in a couple of hours without even a pause. The rock was warm in the sun, the year was fading but for a while we understood what it was all about, why we do what we do.

My 29th birthday, musing over the blank white groove left of *Bastille*, capable of the moves but maybe not the commitment. I placed two bolts, neatly level with the existing pro on its celebrated and run-out neighbour, wary of history and the guy who had once dropped rocks on me whilst I was bolting a different part of the crag. The bolts were too far apart for my fragile psyche that day, but later, when warmer and fitter, *My New Hat* came to life; two grip-clips, 6c moves a long way out, typical High Tor asking the question just one more time. I guess I could have made it popular with a couple more runners, but is that the point? I don't think so, not here, anyway, far above the river.

Malcolm Taylor has been climbing for almost twenty years, and in that time has climbed all over Europe, the UK and North America. His many favourite climbing locations include High Tor, Tuolumne Meadows, the Verdon Gorge, City of Rocks, Raven Tor, and gritstone (on good days). He lives with his wife in Gloucestershire, where they moan about the local crags and drive many miles to avoid climbing upon them.

Above: Mick Carr belays Paul Harrison at the top of Debauchery (E1 5b, 5b), Main Face, High Tor.

Opposite: Paul Harrison takes the Original Route, pitch one (HVS 5a, 5a), Main Face, High Tor.

Above left: *The majestic High Tor, one of the best limestone crags in the Peak District.*

Above and opposite: *Paul Harrison on pitch two of Darius (E2 4c, 5c), Main Face, High Tor.*

Left: *Mick Carr on pitch two of Debauchery (E1 5b,5b), a brilliant climb in a superb position.*

Right: *Mick Carr enjoying the view over Matlock from pitch two of Debauchery (E1 5b, 5b), Main Face, High Tor.*

Below: *Percy Bishton belays Ian Loombe on Flaky Wall (E4 6a), Main Face, High Tor.*

RAVEN TOR

KEITH SHARPLES

Raven Tor's pedigree goes back a long way – to the late '50s and early '60s, when monster aid routes were forced up the centre of the crag. *The Mecca* was perhaps the most famous of this genre. Put up in February 1960 by Graham West and Michael Roberts, it was a landmark. Thirty-eight years later, in October 1998, Steve McClure established the latest landmark with *Mutation*, a 'probable F9a' grade. Still unrepeated, it's the hardest route on the crag and one of the hardest routes in the country. I was privileged to watch Steve do it, just as, fourteen years earlier, I had watched Jerry Moffatt working on the first ascent of *Revelations* (F8a+), the first super hard route in the country. In 1988 Martin Atkinson freed the start of *The Mecca* to give *Mecca; A Mid-Life Crisis* (F8b+) and then two years later Ben Moon bouldered his way up *Hubble* (F8c+). All these routes were 'state of the art' at the time and all remain coveted test-pieces today.

Credentials established, what else does The Snor, as it is known, have to offer? Well, there exists numerous other brilliant and demanding routes, like *Indecent Exposure* (F7b+), *The Prow* (F7b, 7b, 7c) and *Body Machine* (F7c), the latter being one of the best of its grade in the country. Rightwards from here are ten super routes of F8a+ and above, six of which are F8c or harder. So unless, you can crimp and crank like a good-un, boulder to Font 7c/8a, have truly 'gotten inside the red-point thing', and are focused, or just plain talented, then save your skin and send me your chalk.

With me so far? Good, let's move rightwards to where the crag relents and offers some easier routes, the best of which is *Sardine* (F7b+), a steep and strenuous number with a mother of a crux. For some it's a sought-after redpoint whilst for others it's a warm-up route. It's even been soloed! Despite being polished, it remains popular.

Further right The Snor loses height. Behind the bushes hide half a dozen short crimp-nasty horrors, of which *Pump Up The Power* (F8a+) is the best known, although *Boot Boys* (F8a+), with gnarly crimping up a slabby wall of all things, is also a worthy scalp. *Powerband* (F8b), or its extension *Staminaband* (F8b+), are just two of the brilliant boulder traverses hidden by the bushes. Just watch and weep as the locals crank reps of these and other horrors.

Keith has been climbing regularly since 1973. Having spent many days at Raven Tor, he has climbed most of the routes there. He has also climbed as far afield as Thailand and the USA.

Above: *Steve McClure on* Mutation (F9a), *Raven Tor.*

Opposite: *Richard Bingham on* Body Machine (F7c), *Raven Tor.*

Above: *Andy Cave, one of Britain's great all-round mountaineers, on the first of three pitches of the classic route, The Prow, (F7c), Raven Tor.*

Above left: *Sarah Harrison at the end of the hard traverse on the first pitch of Rooster Booster (F7c+), Raven Tor.*

Opposite: *Richard Williams on Revelations (F8b), Raven Tor.*

Left: *Keith Sharples finding his Mecca (F8b+) at Raven Tor.*

THE EASTERN GRITSTONE EDGES

IAN SMITH

Gritstone engenders strong emotions, but love or loathe it it's hard to ignore. The escarpments of the Eastern Edges of the Peak District (Bamford, Stanage, Burbage, Froggatt, Curbar) ride proud on the fringes of the moors high above the Hope and Derwent Valleys, providing high quality climbs of every possible difficulty. The range of routes lies not just in how difficult they are but the way in which they have to be climbed – from superbly protected jamming cracks to virtually blank unprotected slabs and aretes.

West-facing, the Edges provide climbing and bouldering year-round. The cold months provide maximum friction for skin and boot rubber and are the right time to tackle harder routes; while the summer months provide some idyllic moments. But grit is always brutal. Abrasive jams cut viciously into the backs of hands; shoulders and backs twist and distort in extreme stretches between horizontal breaks; feet scream in pain on tenuous smears.

Bamford Edge has probably the best outlook and situation and some of the best routes – but it is one of the least visited crags. The reason – it's on a private grouse moor and is heavily keepered; you should phone for permission before climbing there.

Stanage – four miles long and with more than a thousand routes, offers a lifetime of inspiration and joy. The aptly named Popular End is probably the busiest crag in Britain and queues for the classic routes are likely. Travel to the other extreme, though, past The Plantation, High Neb and Marble Wall to the Northern End and enjoy the solitude and tranquillity of some rarely climbed gems.

Burbage North and South, although sharing a name, couldn't be more different. The North Edge is friendly, the rock quality is superb, most routes are less than Extreme, though there is a smattering of classic desperates. The South Edge is a darker, tougher proposition and includes the Quarry and the Cioch Block; this Edge is currently home to some of the current, top 'hard grit' routes.

Froggatt is another very popular venue – it provides both classic cracks and highly technical slabs, and has one of the Peak's finest Pinnacles providing a dozen routes which finish on a real summit.

Curbar is the joker in the pack. All the routes feel hard for their grade and it can be a debilitating experience, mentally as well as physically. But the quality, if you're up to the challenge, is exceptional.

Ian Smith has been climbing for more than 30 years and has lived in Sheffield for 20 years of that time, a handy 10-15 minutes drive from Stanage. He works as the Deputy Editor of High *magazine and has also long been involved with voluntary work on guidebooks, supplying photos to numerous Peak guides, editing Welsh guides and writing the first ever climbing guide to the island of Jersey.*

Above: *Gritstone means friction, but not always the best of holds.*

Opposite: *Mick Carr on Left Unconquerable (E1 5b), Stanage Edge.*

Left: *Simon Jones takes in the sunset from on top of Stanage Edge.*

Opposite: *Adrian Berry climbing Goliath (E5 6a), Burbage South.*

Bottom left: *Sam Whittaker is keen to be Avoiding the Traitors (E7 6c), Bamford Edge, on the fourth ascent of this route.*

Below: *Mike Lea climbs delicately on the blank slab of Trout (Salmon Left-hand) (E6 6b), Lower Tier, Bamford Edge.*

Right: *Sam Whittaker on* Not to be Taken Away *(E2 6a), the Plantation, Stanage Edge.*

Below: *The internationally renowned German climber, Stefan Glowacz, soloes Crescent Arete (E1 5b), the Plantation, Stanage Edge.*

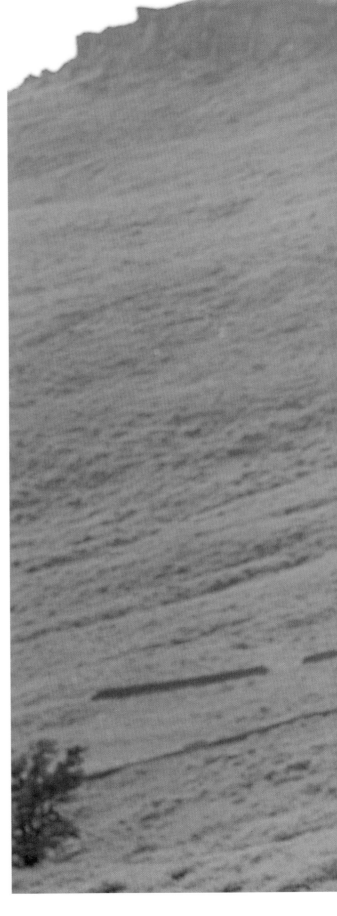

Above: *Mike Lea pulling hard on the first ascent of Dreadnaught (E7 7a), Tower Face area of Stanage Edge.*

Following pages: *Sam Whittaker makes the first 'beta flash' of Slackers (E7 6b), Curbar Edge.*

Above: *Sam Whittaker soloing* Chequers Buttress *(HVS 5b),* Froggatt Edge.

Above right: *Tim Hulley belays Mark Elliot on* Nosferatu *(E6 6b),* Burbage South.

Opposite: *Sam Whittaker belays Seb Grieve on the first ascent of* Strapiotente *(E7 7a),* Froggatt Edge.

Right: *Seb Grieve on the first ascent of* Stretch Armstrong *(E7 6b),* Curbar Edge.

THE ROACHES

SIMON NADIN

Fantastic sculptural forms littered across a surreal landscape. These natural battlements rise out of the Cheshire plain standing against the full onslaught of the prevailing westerlies. Dramatic roofs, striking aretes, pebble-dashed walls and savage cracks all created by the elements in puzzling combinations to give the climber many of the best and most challenging routes on gritstone.

Doing my first climb at The Roaches, I have always had a strong affinity with the area. The feeling of surprising remoteness – for such easily accessible moorlands – and the calming influence I feel while climbing here, constantly brings me back for more. As a youngster, hikes would take me wandering over the Staffordshire Moorlands searching for the elusive Wallabies, passing such attractions as Luds church, The Hanging stone, Sky Line and finally to The Roaches itself. It enjoys sunshine into the late evening and views across to the Welsh hills on fine days. Lines naturally draw the eye and capture the imagination. *Valkyrie* and *The Sloth* both evoke images of heroic pioneers in hob-nail boots and hemp ropes pushing the limits of their day. Surrounded by so many outstanding features it was inevitable to be drawn towards climbing them. One such feature I later discovered to be *Jeffcoat's Chimney*. Stanley Jeffcoat, the first ascensionist, was another Buxton lad who had had that very same urge seventy years prior to my ascent.

The shady aspect of Ramshaw and its more than fair share of ferocious cracks makes it an intimidating prospect. One of my first encounters here was *Don's Crack*, a fierce product of the era. I left beaten and marked by the climb, but with a greater respect for the rock and Don Whillans - who climbed this in the '50s without Friends. Amazing elemental forces have carved its outrageous features like the *Winking Man* and *Ramshaw Crack*, routes of such a beautiful and natural form.

Today climbers of all abilities continue to test their nerve against one of the many routes. The area still holds out some unconquered lines, gems to inspire the imagination, stirring that same imperious desire climbers have felt over the decades, rekindling a natural childhood passion to climb.

Simon Nadin started climbing in 1980 and won the World Cup for competition climbing in 1989 after attending seven events all over the world. New routes include Loculus Lie, *E6 6a, 1983;* Barriers in Time, *E6 6b, 1983;* Painted Rumour, *E6 6b, 1985;* Thing on a Spring, *E6 7a, 1986 (still unrepeated);* Paralogism, *E7 6c, 1987.*

Above: *Gritstone exacts a pound of flesh!*

Opposite: *Sam Whittaker on* The Thin Air (E5 6a), Lower Tier, The Roaches.

Above: *Paul Harrison on Commander Energy (E2 5c), Lower Tier, The Roaches, with the Don Whillans Memorial Hut in the background.*

Left: *Jason Pickles belays John Dunne on the second pitch of Valkyrie (VS 4b, 4c), Lower Tier, The Roaches, one of the best routes on gritstone at this grade.*

Right: *Sam Whittaker does battle with the fierce jamming crack of* The Mincer (HVS 5b), *Lower Tier, The Roaches.*

Above: *Jason Pickles soloing the scary* A Fist Full of Crystals *(E6 6b), Lower Tier, The Roaches.*

Right: *Sam Whittaker on the very serious roof climb of* Paralogism *(E7 6c), Upper Tier, The Roaches.*

Opposite: *Matt Donnelly belaying Ben Tetler on* Round Table *(E1 5a), Upper Tier, The Roaches.*

Below: *Sam Whittaker and his dog Jake, relaxing beneath the Lower Tier of The Roaches.*

PEN TRWYN

LIBBY PETERS

Often viewed as a training ground or poor weather alternative, the limestone cliffs of the Great Orme, Llandudno, are worthy of greater respect and add yet another dimension to North Wales climbing. Historically their development provided an important arena during the grade-pushing 1980s. For many it satisfies the need to scuttle away from the big serious crags and clip a few bolts for awhile. Yet this is not the easy option it may sound. The rock is compact and the climbing fingery, while the routes often feel hard for their grade.

The approach to the crags is undeniably easy. A tolled tourist road snakes around the

Above: *Preparing to climb at Upper Pen Trwyn.*

Opposite: *Lucy Atkinson on Contusion (F6c), Upper Pen Trwyn.*

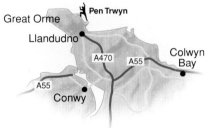

Great Orme headland, dividing the Upper and Lower Pen Trwyn. Car-side climbing is possible but it is perhaps better to park on the fringes of the once prosperous Victorian holiday town and stroll amidst tourists to the crag. After all, the kiss-me-quick hat and candy stalls and the tea-dance music drifting ashore from the Victorian pier, are an essential part of the atmosphere here on the North Wales coast.

If the tides are right, the Lower Pen Trwyn provides a remarkably peaceful and sheltered setting. For those of normal human finger strength with E1-2 (F6a) aspirations, the best crop is bunched at the right-hand end of the crag where bolted lower-offs provide low hassle exercise. Moving left, the crag steepens into compact and fingery E4 (F6c) territory, whilst further left still the neck-craning bulges yield at their weakest to thuggy E5s (F7a). It is on this stretch that the test pieces of their day (*Statement of Youth*, F8a, and *Liquid Amber*, F8c) were put up by Ben Moon and Jerry Moffatt, followed later by Neil Carson's *Big Bang* (F9a). Whichever section you choose to climb on, beware becoming too engrossed and ignoring the sea. The gently lapping waves belie a vicious tide that races in on turned backs.

Out of the reaches of the sea and above the road, Upper Pen Trwyn provides the greatest concentration of routes. Initially the crag faces North East and is at its best on a sunny morning when a South-Westerly gale is blowing. Having escaped the wind-blasting you would be getting elsewhere, you can fully appreciate the tame atmosphere and easy access. Some of the routes are still climbed on natural gear with the bolted routes starting at F6c. Though short, the quality of the rock is excellent and the cafe is never more than a short stroll away.

Libby's climbing experience spans 15 years, at home and abroad. It includes traditional rock, sports and winter climbing, Big Walls, Alpine mountaineering and high altitude expeditions. Libby combines climbing with work around the world as a British Mountain Guide.

Above: *Lucy Atkinson on* Treat Me Like a Person *(F6a+), Upper Pen Trwyn.*

Above left: *Neil Carson on* The Big Bang *(F9a), Lower Pen Trwyn, a route that Ben Moon called 'sick hard'.*

Left: *The left-hand side of Lower Pen Trwyn, home to some of the hardest routes in the country.*

Opposite: *Percy Bishton on* Dive, Dive, Dive *(F7b), Upper Pen Trwyn.*

GOGARTH

GILL LOVICK

On my first visit to Gogarth, I was deposited with a novice climber to do *Puffin*, a rare V Diff, one of my first multi-pitch climbs. It was loose, and my second kept me on an irritatingly tight rope. Having been used to the security of perfect runners and solid rock in the Peak and Llanberis Pass, I said I'd never go back to Gogarth. I was persuaded to return a few years later with Steve, who patiently belayed me as I failed on *The Strand*, E2, having placed my entire rack in the first 40 feet, and not trusted a single runner. Exhausted and miserable, I then had a hard time seconding *Citadel* in scorching heat, carrying a rucksack. Sobbing, I said I'd never return (again!). I was going to stick to easy access, single-pitch, protectable routes. However, a couple of years later, I was given my first taste of Castell Helen, seconding *Free Stonehenge*, E7. I was completely gripped by the whole experience, but perversely enjoyed it; a few weeks after this, I had a scary, mega-belaying session on what was to become *Extinction*, a bold and dangerous route, and the Main Cliff's only E8. Traumatised, I once again vowed never to return, and I meant it this time.

Above: *Pitch one of* Concrete Chimney *(HVS 5a, 5a), Gogarth.*

Opposite: *The eponymous* Gogarth *(E1 4b, 5a, 4c, 4b, 5b).*

But time clouds the memory. With no pressure to second hard routes, I was persuaded to return open-minded to lead some of the more benign routes, building a new relationship with Gogarth. I led *The Strand*, happily this time, and plenty of other memorable routes. So much of the climbing is immaculate; when I did *The Moon*, E3, my eyes were out on stalks – brilliant climbing, brilliant place – I wanted to go back down and do it all over again.

I suppose the reason I kept returning is because Gogarth has so much life. I love climbing by the sea, and the scenery is fantastic. Mousetrap Zawn is made of layers of hard and soft, crumbling rock, folded and re-folded into a confusing mass of lines that invite you to climb

them against your better judgement. When I'm particularly nervous, I allow myself to be diverted by brilliant flowers and lichens, the audience of seals around North Stack, giant spiders on Red Walls, vibrant rock pools, wheeling sea birds, the mesmerising rhythm of the waves and the sun on the south-facing Rhoscolyn.

Gill Lovick was born in Norfolk, so came to climbing late, being persuaded she should be good at it. Gill has been climbing for about 17 years now, starting in the Peak and at Swanage when she lived in the south, eventually moving to Wales in 1987. Gill has been on many ascents of very hard routes with Steve Mayers, some new ones, but usually as a second. She has led loads of E3s and some E4s, a bit harder on bolts, and even gave competition climbing a go for the experience. Gill now co-owns and manages the Beacon Climbing Centre near Llanberis, North Wales.

Above: *Tim Neill on Mainlinin' (E4 6a), Rhoscolyn, Gogarth. This area is a sun-trap in the winter and tempts many folk onto routes on the odd day when the sun shines.*

Opposite: *Paul Harrison belays Chris Hindley on South Sea Bubble (E3 5c), North Stack Wall, Gogarth.*

Right: *Simon Jones on the lip of the big sea cave in a stunning position on Electric Blue (E4 5c), Rhoscolyn, Gogarth.*

Above: *John Codling on the magnificent Magellan's Wall (E4 6a), Rhoscolyn, Gogarth, which takes a line over the lip of the concave wall before ascending the arete.*

Right: *George Smith and Adam Wainwright on the first ascent of Mad Brown, pitch four (E7 6b, 6b, 5b, 6a), Wen Zawn, Gogarth.*

Above: *Glenda Huxter, one of the country's leading women climbers, making the first ascent of Care in the Community (E5 6a), Red Wall Left Hand, Gogarth.*

Below *Paul Harrison on the first pitch of Spider Wall (HVS 5a, 4c), with North Stack Wall in the distance, Wen Slab Area, Gogarth.*

THE LLANBERIS PASS

MALCOLM CREASEY

The Llanberis Pass is steeped in climbing history, a place where generations of climbers with the eye for a line, and more than a little faith, have created a special atmosphere. It was the early British alpinists with tweed jackets and nailed boots who first scrambled amongst the rocks as early as the 1890s. But it was not until forty years later that serious development took place. Then, during the 1950s, exploration gathered pace when Joe Brown produced a string of out-standing routes. Two in particular, *Cenotaph Corner* and *Cemetery Gates*, epitomising the best of 'the Pass' - steep rock, commitment, exposure, and superb climbing.

It is a valley of contrasts – between the north and south side, divided by the road which seems such an intrusion into this wild, mountainous, craggy landscape. Routes on the north side tend to be steep, take good protection, catch the sun and dry quickly; whilst those on the south are less steep, with only adequate gear, and can remain damp for days in the shadow of their sombre gloom. Weather changes affect the mood of the pass considerably, where magic and atmosphere are almost as impor-tant as the rock itself.

No other valley offers such a diversity of routes – hard, easy, short, long, roadside or mountain crag, sunny or sombre, yet always traditional. This is not a place for bolts and pegs. From Cwm Glas Bach where the evening sun dances among hidden gems, to the established classics whose very names are synonymous with the finest of British rock. Across to the south the sparsely protected slabs of Dinas Mot, or mist-shrouded heights of Cyrn Las. Then there are the boulders by Pont y Gromlech if the spirit is lacking or time is short. For my own part, the memories are numerous – that fine sunny week in early September when we did *Erosion Groove*, *Kaisergebirge Wall*, the *Direct*, *Diagonal*, *West Rib*, the *Corner* and the *Gates*. But that was 30 years ago when we were young. Since then there have been many oth-ers, *Main Wall*, the finest Severe in Britain completed in a thunder storm, *The Grooves*, *Plexus*, *Nexus*. I could go on, and hopefully will, because for me 'the Pass' remains a magical place. And then there's the slate...

Malcolm Creasey first climbed in 'the Pass' in the late sixties and has climbed there on a regular basis ever since. He prefers the mountain atmosphere of Cyrn Las where The Grooves *and* Main Wall *are two of his favourite routes. After that, any of the classics on Dinas Mot. He has done the easier routes (*Nea, Crackstone Rib Direct, Western Slabs *etc.) dozens of times through either instructional or guiding work.*

Above: *A view straight up the beautiful and atmospheric Llanberis Pass, North Wales.*

Opposite: *Peter Robins on the second pitch of Spectrum (E2 5b, 5c, 5a, 4b), Clogwyn y Grochan, Llanberis Pass.*

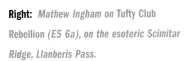

Above: *Tim Emmett on the second ascent of Nightmayer (E8 6c), Dinas Cromlech, Llanberis Pass.*

Right: *Mathew Ingham on* Tufty Club Rebellion (E5 6a), *on the esoteric Scimitar Ridge, Llanberis Pass.*

Right: *Patch Hammond makes the upper moves on* The Bog of the Eternal Stench *(E6 6b), Craig Ddu, Llanberis Pass.*

Following pages: *Peter Robins enjoying Kaisergebirge Wall (HVS 5b), Clogwyn y Grochan, Llanberis Pass.*

Below: *Jamie MacDonald in the groove on Brant Direct (HVS 5a), Clogwyn y Grochan, Llanberis Pass.*

Top: *John Dunne on the crux pitch four of* The Quarryman *(E8 6c, 6b, 6c, 7a/b), Twll Mawr, Llanberis Slate Quarries, first climbed by Johnny Dawes in 1986.*

Above: *Unknown climbers on* The Monster Kitten *(E1 5c), at the most accessible of venues, Vivian Quarry, Llanberis Slate Quarries.*

Opposite: *Peter Robins on the sustained* Geordie War Cry *(E5 6b), Bus Stop area, Llanberis Slate Quarries.*

Left: *Patch Hammond looking at his own reflection on* Bathtime *(E5 6a), Vivian Quarry, Llanberis Slate Quarries.*

TREMADOG

NIGEL SHEPHERD

'Road dry – crag dry' a mate of mine is fond of saying. Surprisingly 99% of the time he's absolutely right. Tremadog is the premier venue when the weather is bad in the mountains of North Wales. However, it offers fine climbing worth seeking out for its own sake, regardless of rain or shine on the higher crags.

Thousands of years ago these cliffs stood guard over a wide estuary leading to the Irish Sea. The millennia and the hand of mankind have claimed back the land and turned it into fertile pasture. Today the rocks are a haven for rare plants and nesting birds and offer a glimpse of ancient Oak Forest once so prevalent in these parts.

From a climber's perspective, the history of development offers an insight into trends in hard technical climbing over the last four decades. With each passing era Tremadog has, uniquely, offered climbers routes of the highest technical standards achieved in Britain. In the '60s, climbs like *Vector* and *Pellagra* were viewed as an audacious prelude to the birth of hard technical climbing in improbable places. In the '70s, the freeing of *Zukator* of its aid points and the ascent of *Fingerlicker* and *The Void* once again proved that limits had not yet been reached. The '80s offered up the now world-renowned *Strawberries*, once one of the hardest climbs anywhere on the globe. Whilst the '90s have not perhaps given up quite so many classic hard climbs, a consolidation of climbing standards has seen many repeats of climbs that were once considered hallowed ground.

But it is not only for hard climbing that Tremadog is known. There are climbs at the Severe and Very Severe grade that are undisputed classics of their genre. How many hundreds of thousands of pairs of hands and feet have passed over climbs like *One Step in the Clouds*, *Christmas Curry*, *Poor Man's Peuterey* or *Creagh Dhu Wall*?

Its popularity is unlikely to diminish, for there are adventures on rock whatever the standard you might seek. Such intense usage is not without environmental consequence and many trees that once stood proudly on high ledges have disappeared and rockfalls occur from time to time as soil is denuded from cracks and crannies. It is our responsibility to tend considerately for nature's ways and to tread with care, leaving Tremadog intact for future generations as we have enjoyed and enjoy it today.

Above: *Craig Pant Ifan, a popular climbing venue at Tremadog.*

Opposite: *Percy Bishton on Spare Rib, pitch two (E4 6a, 6a), Craig Pant Ifan.*

Nigel Shepherd is a British Mountain Guide. He has climbed in many parts of the world, on traditional rock routes, sports routes, and snow and ice. He lives in North Wales and knows the crags and mountains of this beautiful area of Britain intimately.

Above: *Airlie Anderson and Mark Pretty discuss the fourth and final pitch of* Cream *(E3 4c, 5c, 5c, 6a) Craig Bwlch y Moch, Tremadog.*

Right: *Airlie Anderson nearing the top of pitch four of* Cream, *(E3 4c, 5c, 5c, 6a), Craig Bwlch y Moch, Tremadog.*

Above: *Airlie Anderson on Cream, pitch four (E3 4c, 5c, 5c, 6a), Craig Bwlch y Moch, Tremadog. The upper headwall is home to some of the best and hardest routes at Tremadog.*

Right: *Airlie Anderson belays Peter Robins on Neb Direct (E3 6a), Craig Bwlch y Moch, Tremadog, with Eric's Cafe in the background.*

Following pages: *Percy Bishton on pitch two of Scratch Arete, (HVS 4c, 5a,), Craig Pant Ifan, Tremadog. This is one of the finest routes at this grade at Tremadog.*

CADER IDRIS & CRAIG CYWARCH

JOHN SUMNER

A climbing area which is off the beaten track. An area where you can climb three-star routes without another climber to be seen. Where's the catch? Well, the scenery is superb and the wildlife abundant, including the magnificent buzzards and peregrines. At Cywarch there is a certain amount of vegetation – I cannot deny it. Saying this, there are routes which will always be clean, mainly due to their steepness. Gems such as *Shade of Pale* (E1/2), *Dream Racer* (E2), *The Overlap* (E2) and most routes on Tap-y-Gigfan. Certain areas on Cader Idris are also without vegetation, such as the great clean slabs on Cyfrwy with routes such as *Obsession* (VS) and *Gwydrin* (E1).

Over the last ten years, many new crags have been discovered and worked on, mainly by activists Martin Crocker, Terry Taylor and myself. Existing crags have had superb new hard routes added, mostly by Martin, who has completely changed the mid-Wales scene over the last few years. Previously only three E5s existed here (put up by John Codling and Andy Grondowski back in the '80s). Now there are close to a hundred routes ranging from E4 to E7, some rating along with the best in the country.

The area has many classic easier grade routes as well and it is for these that most climbers at the moment come to mid-Wales. There is the classic *Cyfrwy Arete* (Diff), *Obsession* (VS) and *Pencoed Pillar* (HVD) on Cader Idris. In the Cywarch area, you will find such classics as *Will-o-the-Wisp* (HVD), *The Gem* (HS), *Buzzard's Balcony* (S), *Doom* (VS) and *Acheron* (HVS).

Gist Ddu is my favourite mid-Wales crag. It is for the connoisseur, in a fantastic setting on the end of the Aran ridge. It has the best rock in the area. Routes undertaken here will always remain in the memory – *Aardvark* (HVS), a Martin Boysen classic of the '60s; *Voie Suisse* (E1), *Moai Man* (E1) and *Obvious* (HVD).

On these great mountain crags, the independent-minded can really get away from the madding crowds found further north in Snowdonia. Access may not be as convenient, but the rewards and the adventure in splendid isolation are there for the few.

John Sumner regards himself as a Lancastrian although he has spent most of his working life in Stafford (he's a design draughtsman with an engineering firm). A member of the old Rock and Ice Club, where he got the nickname Fritz, he has climbed extensively in the Alps, North Faces being his main objective. He is still climbing North Faces in the Alps in winter after 45 years of climbing. On rock, he climbs E1-E2, and enjoys the bolted routes in all areas from Derbyshire to the South Coast.

Above: *John Ball on Hryib, pitch five (HS 4b, 4a, 4a, 4a, 4a), Cyfrwy, Cader Idris.*

Opposite: *John Sumner on Darker Angel, pitch five (E3 5a, -, 5a, 5c, 5c, 4c), Craig Cywarch.*

Left: *Nigel Turner on The Overlap (E2 5c), a steep and well-protected line on Craig Cywarch, first climbed in 1971 by John Sumner, R. Thorndyke and R.Cully.*

Above: *The imposing cliffs of Cyfrwy high on the northern slopes of Cader Idris, where the slabs and grooves of this massive section of rock blend into the summit ridge of the mountain.*

Right: *Kurt Sumner on* Lanchester *(VS 4b), Craig Cywarch.*

PEMBROKE

DAVE VIGGERS

I thirst for this. It's not a want but a real need - the need to succeed in this arena. The peers are watching. Brown hands reaching for a brown jug, my cracked and bleeding fingers flit across the unyielding glaze, lift, and fail, the weight on my battered forearms just too much. A loud cheer from the throng acknowledges the failure, but there's a gleam in a dark moment; Caris takes pity on me, smiles and pours the tea, and now we are laughing together. The end of the tannin ritual concludes the afternoon break and we race back to the crag for another session.

Forget escapism, climbing is about routine, and especially so in Pembroke. You rise from your alcohol-driven choice - a ditch for the drunk, the chapel for the water-proof, the church doorway for the sinners, all stiff with yesterday's failures, and it starts again. The questing probes to the cliff edge, the hesitant launch over the edge, long probing feet into the moccasins of hell, but there is joy here too. Above is 150 feet of intense experience. Bright, white limestone absorbing your time, your energy, your job, your divorce, your life. You top out sweaty and sunburnt, pumped and purged. The best 15 minutes, sated and elated, while your mate struggles with the weight of your life. Below the sea, above the skylarks and you between, sweat cooling, feet easing back to life - a life momentarily good. United you consult, scheme, pressure, each with his own desires and line for life. The Leap beckons, as it has done nearly every day this summer.

A special place, so public yet once on stage nobody can reach you. Success here is yours alone. At the top your friends pass, elated at your success or stay speech along with the setting sun. A lowering fireball to the west and it's time to go. Stumbling along the track you don't want it to end and yet the ritual is not yet over. Shoulder to shoulder you drink, talk, dissect the day. You try to live the experience of others, knowing that yours is the day, the only way worth noting. You check yourself, rise above it, praise and encourage. The sad, the lonely, the good, the bad, the gifted and the gauche are all there. Different players but the same ritual. World's best - and Caris smiled.

Dave Viggers has been climbing for 30 years on rock and ice throughout Britain and Europe. He has eventually settled on guidebook writing as a way of avoiding the fear, but keeping the Kudos. Bolt climbing bores him and his passion is new routing above the sea - hence his love of the Pembrokeshire coastline.

Above: *Tim Emmett resting after the first ascent of* The Muppet Show (E7 6b), *Rusty Walls, Pembroke.*

Opposite: *Neil Gresham on Lucky Strike (E2 5b), Rusty Walls, Pembroke.*

Above: *John Dunne on his own route, and the hardest in Pembroke,* Big Issue *(E9 6c), Bosherston Head, Pembroke.*

Right: *Richard Brown on* The Gadfly *(VS 4c), Crystal Slabs, Pembroke.*

Opposite: *Unknown climber on* Sea Mist *(HS 4a), Saddle Head, Pembroke, with sea mist rolling in.*

Above: *Alan Leary and Emma Alsford on* Isambard's Kingdom (HVS 5a), *a route with some loose rock and fine surroundings, The Green Bridge Area, Pembroke.*

Left: *Sabina Eggert on the classic two-pitch climb, Trevallan Pillar (E4 6a, 5c), Trevallan, Pembroke.*

Opposite: *Neil Gresham on the superb route,* Lucky Strike *(E2 5b), Rusty Walls, Pembroke.*

GOWER

EMMA ALSFORD

The Kinks must have written *Sunny Afternoon* from a beach on Gower. Or was it Lou Reed with *Perfect Day* from Worm's Head, overlooking the Llangenith surf at sunset. The thing is, I can never recall having had intense climbing days on Gower. I have, however, spent many a lazy sunny afternoon clocking up memorable times amongst friends, with climbing being the central theme – to begin with, anyway...

Gower was the first area in Britian to be designated an Area of Outstanding Natural Beauty and it is the scenic allure of its ragged coastline, jutting prominently from the rest of South Wales, which provides the attraction, as much as the climbing itself. The main stresses of climbing revolve around who has the cool box and deciding when to take the next swim break.

Above: *Horses grazing at Threecliff Bay, Gower.*

Opposite: *Chris Savage on Crime and Punishment (E5 6b), Trial Wall, Rhossili Crags, Gower.*

Gower has the reputation for being a middle grade climbers' paradise, particularly suited to those partial to the gentler angles of vertical motion. It is also more harshly labelled as an inferior Pembroke. Yet for variety and choice, in a picturesque setting, nowhere comes close.

Between Rhossili and Worm's Head one can battle with the short gems of Trial Wall, while the antics of paragliders cruising high overhead help to while away the belaying hours. Take a saunter away from the surfers at Llangenith to the popular Fall Bay Buttress, with its abundance of classic groove lines. For those with a little more spunk, Giant's Cave beckons, with some of the hardest test-pieces on Gower. Whilst on hot, sticky days taste the delights of some deep water soloing nearby. Gower may take you back in time, but it keeps up with modern trends. For there are sports climbing venues also, ranging from the bolted slabs of Barland Quarry to the arm-pumping, gravity-defying clip-ups of Foxhole. But for the true golden sand experience, you are hard pushed to beat the idyllic surroundings of Three Cliffs, with some entertaining climbs straight off the beach. And for those with a phobia for slabs, but a purist approach, few crags master the quality and atmosphere of Yellow Wall. Gower also has plenty of non-tidal options, from the exposed buttresses of Pennard to the sheltered classics of Paviland and Juniper Wall.

There is a soothing tranquillity in the scenic approaches, abundant flora and fauna, and an assortment of activity across the entire peninsula. An ease of access to most cliffs, where few abseils are necessary, add to the serene nature of the climbing here.

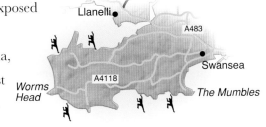

Emma Alsford started climbing in 1988 mainly in Pembroke and has now climbed all over Britain and around the world. Her favourite climbs are on sea cliffs and in the mountains – the longer the climb the better. A bit obsessive about new routing (over 300 to date), her most memorable climb was Underneath the Arches *(E2 5c) in Pembroke. She has also helped endangered Bald Ibises to nest in Morocco and taught the host of the BBC2 Wales Wonder Women to master the sport in 72 hours!*

Right: *Abigail May on* Scavenger (VS 4b), *Threecliffs Bay, Gower, a route of utmost quality.*

Opposite: *Chris Savage belays Rupert Cross on* The Poser (E1 5b/c), *Poser Buttress, Gower.*

Above: *Colin Binks belays Graham Parkes on the first pitch of* Yellow Wall, (E3 5c, 5c), *Yellow Wall, Gower.*

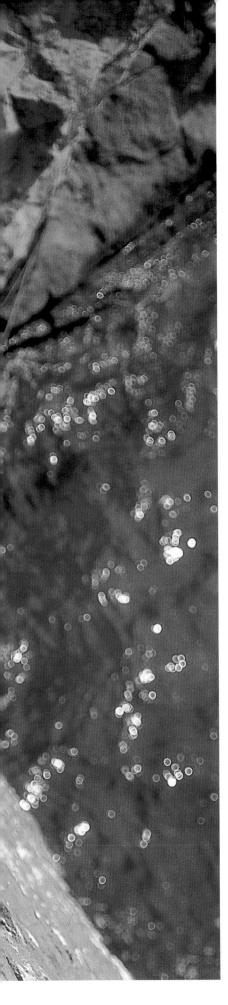

LUNDY

PAUL HARRISON

Twelve miles off the north coast of Devon the granite isle of Lundy stands defiantly across the mouth of the Bristol Channel, its three mile western coast-line exposed to all the elements the Atlantic Ocean can throw at it. Accessible only by a two-hour boat trip or helicopter, a visit to Lundy requires both planning and commitment. Those who persevere however, will be rewarded with some of the finest sea-cliff climbing this country has to offer.

Many climbers visiting Lundy for the first time will, inevitably, be drawn towards the islands most famous rock formation, The Devil's Slide. An ascent of this majestic, four hundred feet sweep of ever-steepening slab seems almost compulsory. The many excellent routes of Landing Craft Bay and The Flying Buttress Area are also popular, whilst those seeking more solitude may venture further north to sample the perfect rock of Arch Zawn or

Above: *Paul Harrison above Torrey Canyon Cliff on the island of Lundy.*

Right: *Dave Savage on Double Diamond (HVS 5b), Flying Buttress Main Cliff, Lundy.*

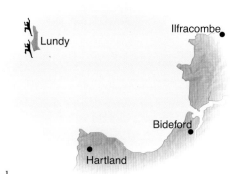

perhaps visit the seals' playground around Phantom Zawn. The more adventurous may prefer to explore Jenny's Cove, a ship's graveyard of a bay, ringed with cliffs of all shape and proportion but dominated by the huge brooding precipice that is The Devil's Chimney Cliff, home to some of the most atmospheric and committing climbs on the island. Lying in the shadow of the cliff but dwarfed by its presence stands The Devil's Chimney, at almost 150 feet, one of the largest and finest sea-stacks in England and Wales. Nearby the dungeon-like recess of Deep Zawn both impresses and intimidates with its sheer, towering walls and its overall sense of confinement. Eventually the cliffs relent, giving way to the more open and aptly named Immaculate Slabs. All around, the cacophony of sea-birds and the roll of an ever-changing ocean add noise, colour and splendour to this most dramatic of coast-lines.

I must have been visiting Lundy for some twenty years now in what for myself and a small group of friends has become something of an annual pilgrimage. In that time I have come to know its many zawns and buttresses intimately, yet its contrasting moods and unique ambience continue to surprise and delight. For me Lundy's greatest attractions are yet to be discovered, the thrill of entering an unexplored zawn for the first time or discovering an unclimbed wall or crack is, when combined with the challenge of climbing out on-sight, both exhilarating and dangerously addictive.

Paul Harrison, age 39, presently lives in Sheffield. He has been climbing for 22 years in Britain, Europe and the States, as well as Japan. He has led up to E5 and currently is climbing about E4. Paul has been involved in over 160 new routes on Lundy as well as new routes in The Peak District, Wales and the South-West.

Above: *An unknown climber on* Mad Axeman (Malloy) (E1 5b), *a thin crack route trending rightwards, Threequarter Buttress, Lundy.*

Opposite: *Mike Snell belaying Paul Harrison over the void on the first ascent of Solaris (E4 6c, 6a), pitch two, Starship Zawn, Lundy.*

Left: *Lundy wildlife – an Atlantic Seal pup off the North coast of the island.*

Above: *Helen Board finding exhilarating exposure on the classic easy climb of Seal Slab (V Diff), Seal Slab, Lundy.*

Right: *Es Tresidder on the delicate pitch one of Ice (E3 5c, 5c), First Buttress North, Lundy. The second pitch changes character, being somewhat more strenuous.*

THE AVON GORGE

MOIRA VIGGERS

Big boys don't cry. There should be an exemption for Avon. I've seen grown men gibber. Come to think of it, I've done a fair bit of gibbering myself. But I'm one of the lucky ones – I learnt to climb there. While abilities in crack climbing, jamming and chimneying may be sadly lacking in my repertoire, like all true Avon aficionados I've developed neat feet, a certain degree of neck and an uncanny ability to levitate over loose blocks. Rising high above you, the polished limestone gleams with Mr Sheen pride – pause to admire your reflection in the hold you are about to use. Communication with your partner is either tactile or telepathic, the traffic noise sees to that. Twenty foot runouts above your last runner are the norm, even in the lower grades. You develop a naive and touching faith in the protective properties of manky old pegs – often that's all there is between you and the tea shack. The 'psychological runner' is an art form. You can spot a 'foreigner' at ten paces – he's the one carrying the full rack of Friends. Surely a No. 4 Friend is fit only for mooring boats, or possibly as an offensive weapon? There ain't no other use for them round these parts.

Am I putting you off? Then think of some of the finest limestone climbing in the country. Fashions come and go, and Avon's heyday may have been some years ago, but goddamit, the place has atmosphere. Emulate the youthful Sir Christian blazing a trail up Main Wall on *Malbogies*, a route years ahead of its time. Adventure across *Pink Wall Traverse*, originally VS and with enough exposure to rival Gogarth's *Dream of White Horses*, lassoing jutting metal spikes for protection as you go – hey after all, this is the wild west country. Test your strength on the Upper Wall above the ramp - nothing here under E2. If your ego needs a boost, head for the natural limestone under the Suspension Bridge – the tourists always like the theatre.

Gone are the days of drug-inspired route names, drunken and debauched 'Bog Wall Dinners', a climbing scene whose leading activists were among the hardest climbers in the country, but the climbs are still here. Avon sits brooding, waiting – the ultimate Urban Myth. Try it. We don't mind if your bottom lip quivers a bit.

Above: *A passing balloon from the festival over the Avon Gorge.*

Opposite: *Dave Viggers on A Dream of Brown Trousers (E2 5b), The Amphitheatre, Avon Gorge.*

Moira discovered climbing late, after moving to the South West. Local limestone provided the basis of a technique somewhat lacking in power and jamming skill, but which has seen some respectable ascents in times now long past. Moira now hides behind work, canoeing, and international jet-setting to avoid climbing, although this is not yet fully successful. Moira dislikes bolts on all rock types and does not own a chalk bag.

Above: *Chris Savage on 5b Wall (E3 5b), Sea Walls, Avon Gorge. This is a serious and unprotected route, usually soloed.*

Right: *Ron Barraclough belaying Chris Savage on the second pitch of* Think Pink *(E3 6a, 5c), Main Wall, Avon Gorge, one of the area's best-known routes.*

Opposite: *Dave Viggers on Simian (HVS 5a), Sea Walls, Avon Gorge.*

DARTMOOR TORS

DAVE HENDERSON

One of my early climbing memories was going to Low Man after school and enjoying *Aviation*, E1 5a/b, in gorgeous light before erecting the tent beneath the crag. A 5.30 am start allowed a view of dawn doing her stuff, shedding light on bits that don't usually have light on. One such light sector was *Vandal and Ann*, a non-juggy HVS on High Man which was followed by the darker *Outward Bound*, a juggy Tom Patey route through a sizeable overhang.

Since then I've climbed most of the routes on Haytor – of particular note were *Interrogation*, E3, with its reasonably safe technical wall climbing; *Haggis*, HVS, on High Man provided a good introduction to soloing and *Rough Justice*, E5, was just dead scary with its fine coating of lichen on the bold top section.

Hound Tor has always been a favourite area and one where the bold will enjoy soloing many of its short routes. The rock, as with most of The Moor, is solid. *Limbo Dancer*, E4, and *Aerobic Wall*, E2, are a couple of favourites but without doubt the most enjoyable is *Suspension Flake*, VS, a fine route for having your photo taken on. A silhouette type shot shows off the positions and if you're lucky will include The Hound of the Basketmeals burger van down in the carpark

And so on to bouldering. Many of the routes at Hound Tor overlap with the bouldering genre. Haytor is a bit bigger but Bonehill Rocks on the road between the two is perfect. I have many superb memories of the place – days when problems feel easy and days when they don't but the most powerful image of the place comes from a winter visit in '96. Early morning pink light coloured fresh snow – very nice, but what made

Above: *Dartmoor ponies grazing at Haytor.*

Opposite: *Stuart Mills on pitch two of* Interrogation *(E3 6a, 5b), Haytor.*

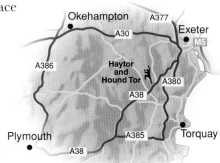

it better was the complete lack of footprints. Empty! Go to the Moor at the weekend in the summer and it'll be heaving but go mid-week in the winter (or some summer evenings) on a crisp clear day and you'll have it to yourself.

Dave Henderson started climbing in the winter of '92–'93 and since then has climbed around the country and made a few trips to France and Spain. Dartmoor is probably his favourite area and he's added a handful of new routes up to E7. Elsewhere he has onsighted E6 and soloed F7c+ with The Mightier *at Anstey's Cove, Torbay.*

Above: *Mark Wakeman belaying Caedmon Mullin on pitch two of Aviation (E1 5b, 5b), Low Man, Haytor, a must-do route for any visitor to the area.*

Right: *Craig Williams soloes the long crack that is Athos (V Diff), Haytor.*

Right: *Caedmon Mullin soloing around on Hound's Head Block at Hound Tor. The routes here are short climbs or long boulder problems – take your pick.*

Opposite: *Chris Fryer near the top of the superb route, Suspension Flake (VS 4c), Hound Tor.*

Below: *Caedmon Mullin on Levitation (VS 4b), Low Man, Haytor.*

CORNISH GRANITE

DES HANNIGAN

I n Cornwall you climb rock with the Atlantic gaping at your back. Cornwall's sea-cliffs rarely rise above 300 feet, yet the sense of exposure created by the vastness of the ocean and by its oceanic sky can set your mind reeling even before you step off the ground. On sea-cliffs there are few points of reference off stage; no hazy valley below your feet, no soft pelt of moorland, no blurred canopy of trees to give a comforting sense of peripheral security. Sea-cliffs engender vertigo from all directions. Look down, and you cope with such everyday exposure. Look outwards, and you feel as if you may be sucked away at any moment into that gaping void of sea and sky.

The solidity of the best Cornish granite compensates for such heart-stopping uncertainty. The granite is peerless on the great cliffs of Bosigran and Chair Ladder and on ocean outcrops such as Sennen. Ropes flicker across a blizzard of feldspar and glittering quartz. Boots lodge reassuringly on wafer-thin edges. Fingers graze across the diamond-hard rock. The void may loom menacingly at your back, but somewhere up ahead, always there is an honest hold, a decent placement.

Granite is a chameleon rock. It is silver and grey beneath dull skies and famously gold in the sun as if its ancient heat still lingers. Its facets are daubed with saffron and lime-green lichens and are stained black and rust-red where rain water bleeds from above and where the sea unloads its salt at the heaving tide-line. Its palette of colours depends on the exceptional Cornish light that takes its piercing clarity and its spectrum from a mirrored sea and sky.

The reality of granite is hard-faced geology of course and climbing on granite is a mechanical mix of technique, strength, control and adrenaline. The romance is in those luminous colours, the sculptural shapes, the scent of the sea on the warm wind, the golden glow beneath a blue sky. Cornish granite combines the best of reality and romance. It may represent a minuscule part of climbing's larger world. Yet, on Cornwall's dwindling peninsula you climb always with an exhilarating sense of freedom inspired by all that nerve-wracking exposure and by the wide world of the ocean itself.

Des Hannigan is a travel writer who has written and contributed to books about such diverse places as Amsterdam and Andalucía, Helsinki and the Hindu Kush. Yet he remains fascinated by the Atlantic coast and cliffs of West Cornwall where he has lived and climbed for many years. He wrote the 1991 and 1992 climbing guides to the area, published by the Climbers' Club.

Above: **Sunset at Carn Galver mine, Bosigran.**

Opposite: **Barnaby Calver on The Variety Show,** *pitch one (HVS 5a, 4c),* **The Great Zawn.**

Right: *Ian Tomlinson belays Renee Allen across the Coal Face on pitch two of Suicide Wall (E1 4b, 5a, 5c, 5a), Bosigran.*

Opposite: *Jodi Vallance on the second pitch of Stone Boom (E2 5b, 5c), Pordenack Point.*

Below: *Martyn Frith abseiling into the Great Zawn to join Barnaby Calver.*

Above: *The well-known South West activist, Mark Edwards, soloing Delilah (E2 5b), Sennen Cove.*

Right: *Brian Stamper on pitch one of Seal Slab (VS 4c, 4b), Chair Ladder, a sea cliff that is home to some of the best low and middle grade routes in the country.*

Opposite: *Andy Dunhill belaying Christine Barbier on Zig Zag (HVS 5a), Sennen Cove.*

CONNER COVE

MIKE ROBERTSON

It's like this – we have choices. Cold days, hot days. With or without ropes. With good friends, vague acquaintances. Planned, maybe on a whim. An evening bash at the local crag, or a little bouldering. All these choices. But always with a smile. This must be the most important factor. Why did we start these things in the first place, if not for the chance of a face-splitter, from ear to ear?

So that's it. With a smile firmly in place. Do we really want ropes? Do they not get in the way, jamming, dragging, confounding? OK, no ropes. But hang on a minute – isn't that a little dangerous? OK, we need a safety net of some sort. Too high for spotters, bouncy castles. How about water, and lots of it; deep, cool, inviting – and just soft enough to provide the freedom we crave?

Welcome to the curious sub-sport of Deep Water Soloing. Let me explain the way things are down here in the far south. We use no ropes (excepting camera work). We carry large quantities of rock boots and chalk bags (you can work that one out for your-self). We seldom look glum, preferring instead to grin amiably as we move across the colourful walls of perfect, fused limestone. We love the sun, and its unruly heat. And, above all, we adore the sea: the feel of it, that post-fall rush of it over our bodies, its enveloping effect. Described by one prominent exponent of the art form as the Green Room, this luscious, fluid monster provides us with everything we need, the opportunity to hide for a brief moment, there-after returning to the guffaws of our pals, and the sunshine once more.

Are things now clearer? We don't always need to succeed – failure, once considered a bum deal, is now deemed part of the pleasure. We don't always need to experience new routes – the old favourites can be considered the very best of old friends.

We hang out, we swim, we enjoy. Could we be thought of as the surfheads of the climbing world? It's possible. It's also possible that we have found an outlet that will ride the test of time, stand as testament to the great English tradition of exploration and discovery. Dorset today, Devon tomorrow. Where will we be next week? Cornwall, Pembroke, Gogarth? Then there's Ireland, the Greek Isles, France's southern coast, Malta, Cyprus, Australia. Will you come and join us?

A former pig farmer and fireman, in the summer months Mike Robertson steps out as a strippergram! Mike's thirst for new sensations has led him to dabble in aid climbing, making the first one day ascent of Laughing Arthur, *and chalk climbing, repeating Neil Gresham's test-piece* Massive Attack. *He hails from Dorset, and says he climbs as often as is humanly possible, tipples the odd beverage and believes the world may yet prove to be flat.*

Above: *Dinghies and rubber rings in the sea off Conner Cove, Swanage.*

Opposite: *Richard Bingham solos Privateer (E6 6b), Funky Wall, Conner Cove.*

Left: *Danny French deep-water soloing on Fathoms (E3 5c), Funky Wall, Conner Cove, Swanage.*

Left: *Leo Houlding surveys the would-be deep water soloists at Conner Cover, Swanage.*

Below: *Crispin Waddy, one of the original deep water soloists, does The Conger (E2 5c), Conner Cove, Swanage.*

Left: *Danny French makes a* Leap of Faith *(E3 5c), Conner Cove, Swanage, during the deep water soloing festival.*

Below: *Jo McLaren soloing* Troubled Waters *(HVS 5a), at Conner Cove, Swanage.*

SOUTHERN SANDSTONE

ROBIN MAZINKE

Tune in, turn up, tie on is very much the laid-back attitude of the Southern Sandstone scene, with Harrison's Rocks at the forefront. This stems from the nature of the rock and style of climbing – top-roping is the norm. There is no leading since placing protection (or even worse – falling on it) would damage the soft rock. Where else in the country could such a climb as *Krait Arete*, 6b(NS), exist? *Krait Arete* is at High Rocks and is possibly the best route on Southern Sandstone, starting with a technical rockover to get established on the arete itself, which is then climbed by a fine series of layback moves to a slightly overhanging finish. However, the important bit is the NS (Not Soloed) part, where the local ethics are such that an ascent can be claimed, even though it has not been soloed.

Climbing on Southern Sandstone is a very social occasion, especially at Harrison's. It is easy to just turn up and join in with a group of mates for a few routes, although all are made welcome by the generally friendly locals. Gear needed is at a minimum, indeed many of the die-hards tie on with a bowline round the waist and use a traditional hand-held belay. Only a sufficiently long sling to ensure that the karabiner hangs over the edge to prevent erosion of the rock is essential. Not that top-roping makes the climbing easy – just the opposite, in fact. Classic climbs such as *Unclimbed Wall*, 5b, *Slim Finger Crack*, 5c, *Monkey's Bow*, 6a, *The Thing*, 6b and *Carbide Finger*, 6c were among some of the earlier routes at their respective grades in the country. The nature of the rock tends towards very rounded, sloping holds so is very good for building strength plus techniques such as foot-locks in horizontal breaks.

The weather in the south-east is amongst the warmest and driest in the country which means that it is possible to climb all year round. But the rock is porous and in some places does take time to dry. Most of the outcrops are in pleasantly wooded areas with amenable short walk-ins. This means that the area is wonderful for summer evenings when it is simple to get out to do a few routes after a day at work before heading for one of the local country pubs for a pint or two of one of the fine Sussex ales.

Robin Mazinke has been climbing for 15 years. He has climbed over 1300 of the routes on Southern Sandstone, which is probably a record. He also climbs in most other areas in the country and particularly likes Peak District gritstone and the sea-cliffs at Pembroke. He also enjoys photography, mountain-biking and drinking beer.

Above: *A busy day at Bowles Rocks. You cannot lead on soft sandstone, hence all the top-roping that goes on at these crags.*

Opposite: *Note that Mike Eden on* Infidel *(6a), High Rocks, is using a top anchor well over the edge of the crag to prevent erosion.*

Infidel! who, with thy finite wisdom,
Wouldst grasp things Infinite, and doest become
A scoffer of God's holiest Mysteries;
Behold this Rock, then tremble and rejoice,
Tremble; for He who form'd the mighty mass,
Could in His Justice, crush thee where thou art;
Rejoice! that still His Mercy spares thee.

J. Phippen.

March 21st 1831.

Right: *Robin Mazinke on the strenuous and overhanging* Birchden Corner (5c), Harrison's Rocks.

Below: *Brian Kavanagh climbing delicately on* Tilley Lamp Crack (6a), High Rocks.

Opposite: *Paul Hayes on* Swing Face (5b), High Rocks.

Following pages: *Seb Grieve soloing* Quietus Right-Hand (E4 6a) *at Stanage Edge in the Peak District.*

GLOSSARY

Abseil Method for descending a rope.

Aid Climbing Mechanically-assisted climbing. Body weight is supported by protection, or other devices, and these are used to directly 'aid' upwards progress.

Alpine climbing, Alpinism Climbing higher peaks or mountains, often involves climbing snow and ice.

Anchor Point where the rope is fastened to the rock.

Arete A jutting prow of rock, an outside corner.

Belay The system using a rope to arrest a climber's fall. Includes the anchors and stance that the 'belayer' uses, and involves using a friction (belay) device to lock-off the rope.

Big Wall A big cliff offering particularly long rock routes, possibly requiring numerous days to climb.

Bolt A construction bolt fixed into a pre-drilled hole as a permanent anchor or protection point.

Bouldering Unroped climbing close to the ground.

Buttress A large protruding section of cliff.

Chalk Gymnast's chalk used to dry sweating fingertips for better grip.

Chimney A body-sized crack, or bigger.

Crag A smaller cliff or set of cliffs.

Crux The most difficult section of the climb.

Face A steep open section of cliff.

Free, free climbing Climbing using hands and feet (and any other body parts) to climb rock's natural features. The rope and protection are there, but are not used to 'aid' the ascent.

Flash To lead climb a route on the very first attempt but with some prior knowledge of the difficulties or sequence of moves.

Flake A semi-detached plate of rock.

Friend Protection device that expands into a crack.

Grade A subjective rating of the difficulties of the climb. There are different grading systems for aid climbs, free climbs, and boulder problems. See p159 for comparisons with other countries' grading systems.

Ground-up To climb from ground level without previously inspecting or preparing the route. As opposed to 'top-down'.

Jam A climbing technique where hand or foot is squeezed inside a crack to provide a hold.

Karabiner Metal alloy snaplinks used to connect the rope to protection and anchor points.

Lead To climb up first from the ground, without rope from above.

Multi-pitch A longer route which is climbed in sections (pitches).

Natural protection Non-permanent protection devices that can be easily placed and removed (not bolts or pitons).

Nut Metal wedge-shaped protection device that is inserted into cracks.

Offwidth A wide crack, awkward to climb.

On-sight An ethically pure free climbing style. The climb is lead climbed 'ground-up' on the first attempt, without any falls or pulling on gear, and without any prior knowledge of the moves.

Overhang An extra steep ('overhanging') section of rock.

Pitch A section of cliff which is climbed between belay points.

Peg or piton Metal protection device (hammered into cracks).

Project An attempted climb, not yet properly free climbed.

Protection The many different types of equipment attached to the rock as anchors to stop a falling climber. Includes 'Friend' devices, metal wedges (wires, nuts, RPs, stoppers and hexes), nylon slings, pitons and bolts.

Pockets Holes in the rock face.

Quickdraw Two karabiners joined by a short nylon sling.

Redpoint A style of climbing, widely regarded as the minimum ethical standard for a 'free' ascent. The route must be lead climbed without a fall or any assistance from the rope or protection.

Roof A horizontally-overhanging section of rock.

RP A brand of very small brass protection nuts.

Runner, running belay The protection point or anchor placed on the climb by the lead climber. The lead climber's rope 'runs' through a karabiner connected to the protection, hence 'runner'.

Runout The distance the lead climber is above their last piece of protection. A 'runout' climb is one with big fall potential.

Second The climber who ascends the pitch after the lead climber.

Slab A large off-vertical sheet of rock, often climbed with balance and friction techniques.

Solo To climb alone – in free climbing this means without a rope ('free solo'); in aid climbing a rope is used ('aid solo').

Sport climbing Where the emphasis is on gymnastic movement and permanent fixed protection.

Top-rope To climb with the rope belayed or anchored from above.

Traditional climbing, trad An ethic with the emphasis on ground-up, where natural protection and route finding skills are required.

Traverse To climb sideways.

Wire, wires A protection nut connected with swaged wire cable.

Zawn Where sea-cliffs form a narrow steep-sided bay.

INTERNATIONAL GRADING TABLE

UK	UK TECH	AUSTRALIAN	FRENCH	US
HS	4a	14	4	5.7
	4b	15	5a	5.8
VS	4c	16	5b	
	5a	17	5c	5.9
HVS		18	6a	
	5b	19	6a+	5.10a
E 1	5c	20	6b	5.10b
E 2		21	6b+	5.10c
				5.10d
E 3	6a	22	6c	5.11a
E 4		23	6c+	5.11b
	5c	24	7a	5.11c
E 5			7a+	5.11d
		25	7b	5.12a
		26	7b+	5.12b
E 6	6c	27	7c	5.12c
		28	7c+	5.12d
E 7		29	8a	5.13a
	7a	30	8a+	5.13b
E 8		31	8b	5.13c
		32	8b+	5.13d
E 9		33	8c	5.14a
	7b		8c+	5.14b
				5.14c

ACKNOWLEDGEMENTS

Creating a book like this is never easy. I would like to extend my heartfelt thanks to the following people, without whose generous and freely given hospitality, help and time, this project would have been nigh on impossible: Renee Allen, Airlie Anderson, Lucy Atkinson, Keith Ashton, Ron Barraclough, Neil Bentley, Adrian Berry, Richard Bingham, Dave Birkett, Percy Bishton, Ben Bransby, Barnaby Calver, Mick Carr, The Climber's Club, Lucy Creamer, Martin Crocker, Rupert Cross, Steve Crowe, Adam Dewhurst, Russel Dicks, Matt Donnelly, Ritchie Duffy, John Dunne, Mark Edwards, Tim Emmett, Helen Fawcett, Nick Fletcher, Neil Foster, Danny French, Martin Frith, Adrian Gibb, Stefan Glowacz, Neil Gresham, Seb Grieve, Patch Hammond, Paul Harrison, Sarah Harrison, Dave Henderson, *High* magazine, Chris Hindley, Adam Hocking, Mary Jenner, Simon Jones, Mike Lea, Graham Lee, Ian Loombe, Steve McClure, James McHaffie, Karin Magog, Abigail May, Caedmon Mullin, *On The Edge* magazine, Gareth Parry, Jason Pickles, Eve Prickett, George Rea, Mike Robertson, Peter Robins, Mike Roch, Keith Sharples, Mike Snell, Brian Stamper, Graham Sutton, Ben Tetler, Ian Tomlinson, Iain Turnbull, Chris Savage, Jodi Vallance, Ian Vickers, Dave and Moira Viggers, Mike Weeks, Sam Whittaker, Craig Williams and Richard Williams. My apologies to anybody I've missed.

My sincere gratitude goes to New Holland, in particular Mike Unwin and Jo Hemmings, for trusting in my abilities, and Alan Marshall for his excellent design work.

For their major contributions to this book, a huge thank you is also due to the following: the writers of each section; the editor Neil Champion for his excellent introduction and all his work on the text; Ron Fawcett, an icon and inspiration, for his superb foreword; Simon Cardy, Chris Craggs, Ron Kenyon, Alan Leary, Simon Nadin, Stephen Reid, Carl Ryan, Don Sargeant, Nigel Shepherd, Keith Sharples, Ian Smith, Sam Sturgess, John Sumner, Dave Wilkinson and Ray Wood for their fine photographs.

Thank you also to Mammutt Ropes, Beyond Hope, Prana, Metolius and Five Ten for supplying climbing equipment and clothing that made my job a whole lot safer. In the field, photographic equipment takes a great deal of punishment, and the generosity and expertise of Harrison Cameras, Sheffield, has been a tremendous help. RCL, Sheffield processed my film with their usual professionalism.

I am grateful to Dave Vincent and Alex Thackway for introducing me to climbing many years ago, and to all the people with whom I have experienced wonderful times in the hills and on the crags.

Many people have offered encouragement and invaluable advice. I am indebted to these people and this book, I hope, is a fitting tribute to all that they saw in me. In particular, my family, Ian Smith for his guidance, and my friends who have patiently listened when the only subject was the book - they know who they are.

Thank you to everyone for sharing my vision.

Finally, I would like to dedicate this book personally to someone who meant the world to me, and through whose courageous battle for life I have drawn great strength - my late sister, Lisa, an angel in the stars.

INDEX